THE GREATEST PLAYERS

GOLF

Steve Goldsworthy

MEDIA ENHANCED BOOKS
AV2 BY WEIGL
ADDED VALUE • AUDIO VISUAL

www.av2books.com

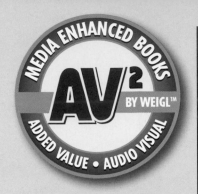

AV^2 provides enriched content that supplements and complements this book. Weigl's AV^2 books strive to create inspired learning and engage young minds in a total learning experience.

Your AV^2 Media Enhanced books come alive with...

Audio
Listen to sections of the book read aloud.

Key Words
Study vocabulary, and complete a matching word activity.

Video
Watch informative video clips.

Quizzes
Test your knowledge.

Go to **www.av2books.com**, and enter this book's unique code.

Embedded Weblinks
Gain additional information for research.

Slide Show
View images and captions, and prepare a presentation.

BOOK CODE

P793558

Try This!
Complete activities and hands-on experiments.

... and much, much more!

AV^2 by Weigl brings you media enhanced books that support active learning.

Published by AV^2 by Weigl
350 5th Avenue, 59th Floor
New York, NY 10118
Website: www.av2books.com   www.weigl.com

Library of Congress Cataloging-in-Publication Data
Goldsworthy, Steve.
  Golf / Steve Goldsworthy.
    p. cm. -- (The greatest players)
Includes index.
ISBN 978-1-62127-502-2 (hardcover : alk. paper) -- ISBN 978-1-62127-505-3 (softcover : alk. paper)
1. Golfers--Biography--Juvenile literature. I. Title.
GV964.A1G65 2013
796.3520922--dc23
[B]
                    2012044834

Printed in the United States of America in North Mankato, Minnesota
1 2 3 4 5 6 7 8 9 0 17 16 15 14 13

032013
WEP300113

Project Coordinator Aaron Carr
Editor Steve Macleod
Art Director Terry Paulhus

Photo Credits
Every reasonable effort has been made to trace ownership and to obtain permission to reprint copyright material. The publishers would be pleased to have any errors or omissions brought to their attention so that they may be corrected in subsequent printings.

Weigl acknowledges Getty Images as its primary image supplier for this title.

Contents

Introduction

The world of professional sports has a long history of great moments. The most memorable moments often come when the sport's greatest players overcome challenging obstacles. For the fans, these moments come to define their favorite sport. For the players, they stand as measuring posts of success.

Golf was invented in Scotland more than 550 years ago. There have been many great players and great moments during the game's long history. These moments include Byron Nelson winning 18 tournaments in one year and Tiger Woods winning **The Masters Tournament** in 1997 when he was 21. Golf has had several of these moments, when the sport's brightest stars accomplished feats that ensured they would be remembered as the greatest players.

Teeing Off

Golf is played by hitting a ball with a golf club into a hole in as few shots as possible. Each time a golfer hits the ball, it counts as a stroke. A golfer begins each hole from the **tee** box. Using a club, a golfer hits the ball from the tee box toward the **putting green**. This area of grass has a hole in the ground marked by a flag. When a golfer hits his or her ball into the cup, the hole is complete.

A game of golf is called a round. A typical round of golf is 18 holes. The golfer with the lowest score at the end of 18 holes wins the round. Golf tournaments can be made up of more than one round.

Gary Player recorded the lowest score ever in a professional golf tournament when he shot a 59 at the 1974 Brazilian Open.

The Golf Course

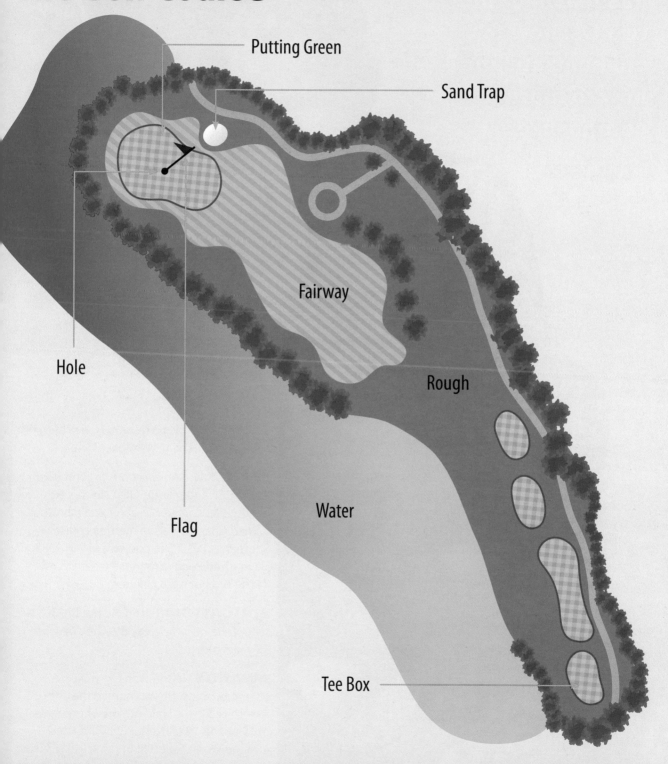

Putting Green

Sand Trap

Hole

Fairway

Rough

Flag

Water

Tee Box

"Every great player has learned the two Cs: how to concentrate and how to maintain composure."

Byron Nelson

Byron Nelson's good sportsmanship earned him the nickname "Lord Byron."

Player Profile

BORN John Byron Nelson, Jr. was born on February 4, 1912, in Waxahachie, Texas.

FAMILY Nelson was born to John Byron Nelson, Sr. and Madge Allen Nelson. He had a sister named Margaret and a brother named Charles. Nelson married Louise Shofner in 1935. She passed away in 1985. He married Peggy Simmons when he was 74. He did not have children.

EDUCATION Nelson did not finish school. He became a **caddy** when he was 12 years old.

AWARDS Nelson won five major championships. He was named the Associated Press Male Athlete of the Year in 1944 and 1945. Nelson was inducted into the World Golf Hall of Fame in 1974. He won the **Professional Golfers' Association (PGA) Tour** Lifetime Achievement Award in 1997.

Byron Nelson
Turned pro: 1932

Early Years

Byron Nelson moved with his family to Fort Worth, Texas, when he was 11 years old. Soon after, Nelson became ill with typhoid fever. His weight dropped by almost half.

The next year, Nelson became a caddy at the Glen Garden Country Club. At the time, caddies were not allowed to play golf at the club. Nelson practiced golfing at night. He placed a white handkerchief over the hole so he could see it in the dark. The country club later changed its rules to allow caddies to play golf. In 1927, Nelson won the country club's caddy championship at age 14. He defeated Ben Hogan by one stroke in a nine-hole playoff at this tournament. Nelson continued to practice and improve his skills. He became a professional golfer in 1932.

Developing Skills

In 1935, Nelson became the **club professional** at the Ridgewood Country Club in New Jersey. Golf equipment was changing at the time. Players were starting to use golf club **shafts** made from steel instead of wood. Nelson developed a new swing to use with the new clubs. He used his legs to help create more power when the golf club was swung down toward the ball. Other professionals started to use Nelson's golf swing. It is still the basic golf swing taught today. Nelson is sometimes called the inventor of the modern golf swing.

Nelson's first important win was the New Jersey State Open in 1935. In 1937, he won his first major championship at The Masters. He won the tournament again in 1942. In 1939, Nelson won the **U.S. Open**, and he won the **PGA Championship** in 1940 and 1945. He won 61 tournaments, including 54 PGA event before retiring in 1946.

Byron Nelson

Greatest Moment

In 1945, Nelson set a record by winning 18 PGA tournaments in one year. He also set a record that year by winning 11 tournaments in a row. He played in a total of 30 tournaments in 1945. He also set a record that year for the lowest score over 18 holes, with 62. He set another record during the season for the lowest score over 72 holes, with 259. Both records have since been broken.

Nelson's average score for 18 holes during 1945 was 68.33. It was a record that lasted until 2000. That year, Tiger Woods' average score for 18 holes was 68.17.

Byron Nelson was awarded the Congressional Gold Medal in October 2006. It was less than one month after he passed away on September 26, 2006. The medal is one of the highest honors an American civilian can receive.

> "The mark of a great player is in his ability to come back. The great champions have all come back from defeat."
>
> Sam Snead

Sam Snead earned the nickname "Slammin' Sam" for his powerful golf swing.

Player Profile

BORN Samuel Jackson Snead was born on May 27, 1912, in Ashwood, Virginia.

FAMILY Snead was born to Harry and Laura Snead. He was the youngest of six children. Snead married his wife Audrey in 1940. They had two sons named Sam Jr. and Terry.

EDUCATION Snead graduated from Valley High School.

AWARDS Snead won seven major championships. He was named the PGA Player of the Year in 1949. Snead won the **Vardon Trophy** four times. He was inducted into the World Golf Hall of Fame in 1974. Snead won the PGA Tour Lifetime Achievement Award in 1998.

Sam Snead

Turned pro: 1935

Early Years

Sam Snead grew up on a farm in Ashwood, Virginia. He became interested in golf when he was 7 years old. Snead first learned how to golf using clubs his father made from tree branches. He practiced golfing at the family farm using a chicken coup and other buildings as **hazards**. Snead soon got a job as a caddy at The Homestead golf course just 3 miles (4.8 kilometers) from the farm. By age 10, Snead was sneaking onto The Homestead golf course at night with his brothers to golf. When he was 17, Snead started working at The Homestead golf shop repairing golf clubs. He became an assistant professional at the golf club at age 19.

Developing Skills

In 1935, Snead played in his first tournament at The Homestead's nine-hole course. He finished in third place, behind two U.S. Open champions. Then, he became the club professional at Greenbrier in White Sulfur Springs, West Virginia. He joined the PGA Tour the next year in 1936. Snead won his first big event that year at the West Virginia Closed Pro tournament.

Snead became known for his long drives and accurate shot. He won his first major tournament at the PGA Championship in 1942. He went on to win the event two more times. He won The Masters three times. Snead won golf tournaments in six straight decades. In total, he won more than 140 tournaments around the world. During his career, Snead won 82 PGA events. This is a record for most career wins in the PGA.

Sam Snead

Greatest Moment

One of Snead's greatest victories was at The Masters in 1954. He was tied with Ben Hogan after 72 holes. Snead scored a 70 in the 18-hole playoff to win the tournament by one **stroke**. It was Snead's last major championship victory during his career.

In 1938, Snead won the Greater Greensboro Open for the first time. He won the event for the eighth time in 1965. That victory set a PGA record for most wins at one event during a career. He was 52 at the time, which is also a record for the oldest player to win a PGA Tour event.

Sam Snead won the Senior PGA Championship six times between 1963 and 1973.

> **"Competitive golf is played mainly on a five-and-a-half-inch course...the space between your ears."**
>
> Bobby Jones

Player Profile

BORN Robert Tyre Jones, Jr. was born on March 17, 1902, in Atlanta, Georgia.

FAMILY Jones was born to Robert Purmedus Jones and his wife Clara. He was an only child. Jones married Mary Rice Malone in 1924. They had three children: Clara, Robert, and Mary Ellen.

EDUCATION Jones attended the Georgia Institute of Technology, Harvard College, and Emory University Law School.

AWARDS Jones won 13 major championships. He was named captain of the World Amateur Team Championships in 1958. Jones was inducted into the World Golf Hall of Fame in 1974.

Bobby Jones served as a captain in the U.S. Air Force during World War II.

Bobby Jones
Amateur golfer

Early Years

Bobby Jones had poor health as a young boy. He started playing baseball and golf to build up his strength. He won his first children's tournament when he was 6 years old. Jones won his first important tournament at the Georgia State Amateur Championship at age 14. That year, he became the youngest player to compete in the U.S. Amateur Championship. He made it to the third round.

Jones continued to practice with his father and golf professional Douglas Edgar. He soon began competing against professional golfers in international competitions. Jones was 18 when he qualified for his first U.S. Open tournament in 1920. He played the first two rounds with golf legend Harry Vardon.

Developing Skills

Between 1916 and 1923, Jones did not win a championship. From 1923 to 1930, Jones won 13 of the 21 major championships he entered. He won his first U.S. Open in 1923. In 1926, he became the first golfer to win the U.S. Open and the **British Open** in the same year. A **ticker tape parade** was held that year for Jones in New York City.

Jones won the U.S. Open four times. He is tied with four other golfers for most career wins at that tournament. Jones won the U.S. Amateur Championship five times, which is a record for most career wins at the tournament. Jones won the U.S. Amateur, the U.S. Open, the British Open, and British Amateur in 1930. He is the only golfer to win all four of these events. Jones retired from golf that year at the age of 28.

Bobby Jones

Greatest Moment

Jones was known for his sportsmanship. During the 1925 U.S. Open, he hit a ball into the **rough**. Jones accidentally brushed the ball with his club when he was preparing to take his shot. He told the official that he was taking a one-stroke penalty for touching the ball. Jones lost the tournament in a playoff. The penalty cost Jones the championship, but his honest scoring earned him the respect of other golfers.

Bobby Jones created The Masters Tournament. The first event was played in 1934 at the Augusta National Golf Club in Augusta, Georgia. Jones also helped design the golf course.

> "There is no tragedy in missing a putt, no matter how short. All have erred in this respect."
>
> Walter Hagen

Walter Hagen was the first golfer to win more than $1 million in prize money.

Player Profile

BORN Walter Charles Hagen was born on December 21, 1892, in Rochester, New York.

FAMILY Hagan was born to William Hagen and Louise Balko. He had four sisters. Hagen married Margaret Johnson in 1917. They had one son named Walter Jr., but divorced in 1921. In 1924, he married Edna Strauss. They divorced in 1934.

EDUCATION Hagen left school when he was 12 years old. He jumped out of a window and headed straight for a golf course.

AWARDS Hagen won 11 major championships. He was inducted into the World Golf Hall of Fame in 1974.

Walter Hagen

Turned pro: 1916

Early Years

Walter Hagen grew up in Rochester, New York. He learned the value of hard work from his father, who was a **blacksmith**. Hagen started working as a caddy at the Country Club of Rochester as a teenager. Hagen played as much golf as he could when he was not working. He began to develop strong golf skills and became the club's assistant golf professional in 1907. Hagen played in his first professional tournament in 1912. He finished in 11th place.

Hagen was also a skilled baseball player. In 1914, he was offered a **tryout** with a professional baseball team. The tryout with the Philadelphia Phillies was at the same time as the U.S. Open. Hagen decided to skip the baseball tryout to play in the golf tournament. In the first round, he set a U.S. Open record by shooting a 68. Hagen went on to win the tournament. It was his first major championship victory.

Developing Skills

Hagen became the first head golf professional at the Oakland Hills Country Club in Michigan. In 1919, he decided to stop working as a club professional. Hagen wanted to spend all his time playing in golf tournaments and events. He became the first full-time tournament professional golfer.

In 1922, Hagen became the first American to win the British Open. He won the tournament four times during his career. Hagen won the PGA Championship five times. He won that tournament in 1921, 1924, 1925, 1926, and 1927. Hagen is thought to be one of the greatest **match play** golfers of all time. He once won 22 straight 36-hole matches. Between his first round in 1921 and his fourth round in 1928, Hagen won 32 out of 33 matches.

Walter Hagen

Greatest Moment

One of Hagen's best-known golf games was a 1926 match play competition against Bobby Jones. The contest was played over 72 holes. With 11 holes left in the competition, Hagen was in the lead by 12 holes. He earned $7,600 by winning the event.

In 1927, a golf team from the U.S. was formed to play in a tournament against a golf team from Great Britain. The tournament would be held every two years. Hagen was the captain of the first six American teams. The international event became known as the **Ryder Cup**.

Walter Hagen retired from competitive golf in 1940. He won 75 tournaments and played in more than 2,500 events during his career.

"I always outworked everybody. Work never bothered me as it bothers some people."

Ben Hogan

Ben Hogan served in the U.S. Army for three years during World War II. After the war, he won his first major tournament at the PGA Championship in 1946.

Player Profile

BORN William Ben Hogan was born on August 13, 1912, in Dublin, Texas.

FAMILY Hogan was one of three children born to Chester and Clare Hogan. He married Valerie Fox in 1935. The couple never had children.

EDUCATION Hogan became a professional golfer at age 17.

AWARDS Hogan won nine major championships. He won the Vardon Trophy in 1940, 1941, and 1948. He was the PGA Player of the Year in 1948, 1950, 1951, and 1953. Hogan was named the Associated Press Male Athlete of the Year in 1953. He was inducted into the World Golf Hall of Fame in 1974.

Ben Hogan
Turned pro: 1930

Early Years

Ben Hogan had a challenging childhood. His father died when Hogan was 9 years old. The family moved to Fort Worth, Texas, shortly after the tragedy. Hogan and his siblings each took jobs to help their mother. At age 12, Hogan became a caddy at the Glen Garden Country Club. Hogan came in second to Byron Nelson at the country club's caddy championship in 1927.

In 1930, Hogan became a professional golfer. He was 17. Unable to control his **hook**, he found it hard to win. Hogan continued to practice his swing, but he had little success as a professional for several years. Hogan almost quit golfing in 1938.

Developing Skills

In 1938, Hogan finished in fifth place at The Oakland Open in California. He earned $285 in the tournament. It was enough to keep his professional career going. After the tournament, Hogan got a job as a club professional in New York. He won his first PGA tournament the same year at the Hershey Four-Ball event.

Hogan won the U.S. Open four times. He won the event for the third time in 1951 at the Oakland Hills Country Club in Michigan. The course was designed to be especially difficult for the tournament that year. Hogan shot a 67 in the final round to win the event by two strokes. Between 1945 and 1949, Hogan won 37 tournaments. He won more money than any other player on the PGA Tour in 1940, 1941, 1942, 1946, and 1948. From 1938 to 1959, Hogan won 64 professional golf tournaments.

Ben Hogan

Greatest Moment

In 1949, Hogan and his wife Valerie were severely injured in a car accident. They were involved in a head-on collision with a Greyhound bus. Doctors told Hogan he might not be able to walk again. The next year, he won the U.S. Open in an 18-hole playoff against two other golfers.

Hogan's greatest season was in 1953. He won five of the six tournaments he entered and became the first player to win three major championships in one year. He was named the PGA Player of the Year and Associated Press Male Athlete of the Year in 1953.

Between 1946 and 1956, Ben Hogan finished in the top 10 at the U.S. Open every year. He won four times, finished second two times, finished third once, finished fourth once, and finished sixth two times.

Arnold Palmer's fans are known as "Arnie's Army."

"The most rewarding things you do in life are often the ones that look like they cannot be done."

Arnold Palmer

Player Profile

BORN Arnold Daniel Palmer was born on September 10, 1929, in Latrobe, Pennsylvania.

FAMILY Palmer was born to Milford and Doris Palmer. He has one brother, named Jerry, and two sisters, named Lois Jean and Sandra. Palmer married Winifred Walzer in 1954. They had two daughters, Peggy and Amy. Winifred died from cancer in 1999. Palmer married Kathleen Gawthrop in 2005.

EDUCATION Palmer attended Wake Forest University.

AWARDS Palmer won seven major championships. He won the Vardon Trophy in 1961, 1962, 1964, and 1967. He was the PGA Player of the Year in 1960 and 1962. Palmer was named the Associated Press Athlete of the Decade for the 1960s. He was awarded the PGA Tour Lifetime Achievement Award in 1998. Palmer was inducted into the World Golf Hall of Fame in 1974.

Arnold Palmer

Turned pro: 1954

Early Years

Arnold Palmer was born in Latrobe, Pennsylvania, about 40 miles (64 km) southeast of Pittsburgh. His father worked as a golf professional and groundskeeper at the Latrobe Country Club from 1921 to 1976. Palmer became a caddy at the country club at age 11.

Palmer won the Pennsylvania high school golf championship twice. He won the West Penn Amateur Championship when he was 17 years old. Palmer joined the Wake Forest University golf team, but left in his senior year. He then spent three years working for the United States Coast Guard. Palmer returned to university and won the U.S. Amateur Championship in 1954. He became a professional golfer that same year.

Arnold Palmer

Greatest Moment

Palmer began the final round in 15th place at the 1960 U.S. Open. He was seven strokes behind the leader. Palmer hit his first shot of the final round 340 yards (311 meters) and landed on the green. He shot a 30 on the first nine holes that day. Palmer finished the day with a score of 65 to win the tournament by two strokes. It was his only victory at the U.S. Open.

Developing Skills

Palmer won his first professional tournament at the Canadian Open in 1955. He won at least one PGA Tour event every year from 1955 to 1971. Between 1960 and 1963, Palmer won 29 PGA Tour events. They included five of his major championships. He won The Masters in 1960 and 1962, the U.S. Open in 1960, and the British Open in 1961 and 1962.

Palmer won 92 professional championships during his career, including 62 PGA Tour events. He won more money than any other player on the PGA Tour in 1958, 1960, 1962, and 1963. In 2004, Palmer played in The Masters for the last time. It was his 50th appearance at the tournament.

In 2004, Arnold Palmer was awarded the Presidential Medal of Freedom. In 2009, he became the second golfer and only the sixth athlete to earn a Congressional Gold Medal.

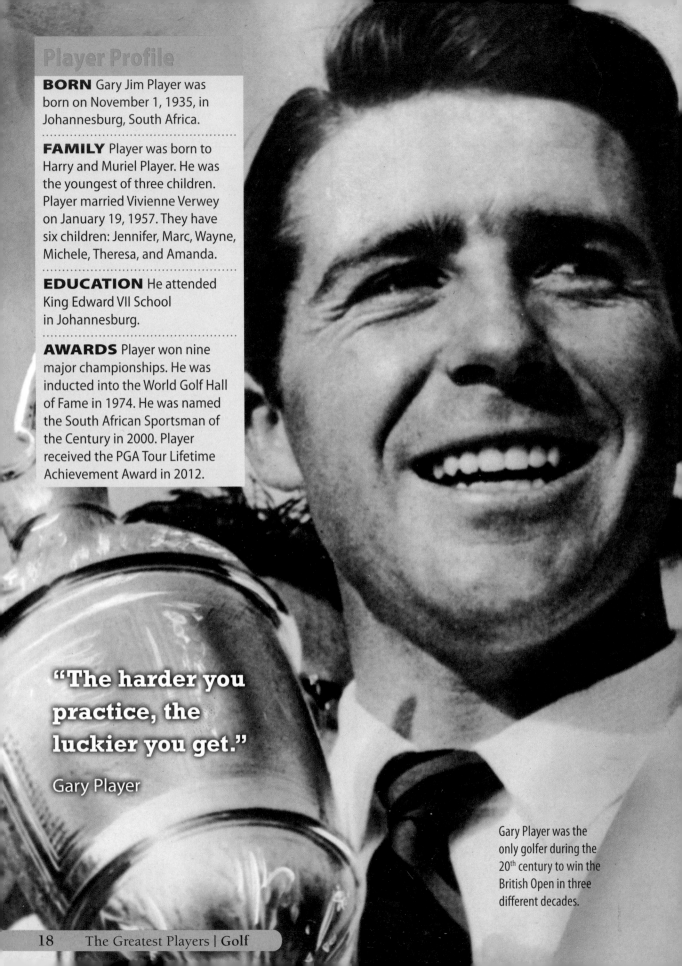

Player Profile

BORN Gary Jim Player was born on November 1, 1935, in Johannesburg, South Africa.

FAMILY Player was born to Harry and Muriel Player. He was the youngest of three children. Player married Vivienne Verwey on January 19, 1957. They have six children: Jennifer, Marc, Wayne, Michele, Theresa, and Amanda.

EDUCATION He attended King Edward VII School in Johannesburg.

AWARDS Player won nine major championships. He was inducted into the World Golf Hall of Fame in 1974. He was named the South African Sportsman of the Century in 2000. Player received the PGA Tour Lifetime Achievement Award in 2012.

"The harder you practice, the luckier you get."

Gary Player

Gary Player was the only golfer during the 20th century to win the British Open in three different decades.

Gary Player
Turned pro: 1953

Early Years

When Gary Player was 8 years old, his mother died from cancer. Losing his mother at a young age motivated Player to try his hardest at everything he did. He started golfing at age 14. He became a professional four years later in 1953. His first big victory as a professional came two years later at the 1955 East Rand Open in South Africa.

Player continued winning at tournaments throughout Africa, Australia, and Europe. In 1957, he played in his first tournament in the United States. The next year, he won his first PGA Tour event at the Kentucky Derby Open. He also finished in second place at the U.S. Open in 1958.

Developing Skills

After joining the PGA Tour in 1957, Player continued to play in other international events. He won 13 professional tournaments that were not part of the PGA Tour between 1957 and 1959. In 1959, Player won the British Open by two strokes. It was his first victory at a major championship.

Player won 165 tournaments around the world during five decades of playing golf. He won 24 of those tournaments on the PGA Tour. Player won more money than any other player on the PGA Tour in 1961. He set a record by winning at least one tournament for 28 years in a row. Player has won nine major championships since joining the Champions Tour in 1985. This series of tournaments is for PGA players older than 50. He won the Senior PGA Championship in 1986, 1988, and 1990. He won the Senior Players Championship in 1987, the Senior British Open in 1988, 1990, and 1997, and the U.S. Senior Open in 1987 and 1988.

Gary Player

Greatest Moment

Player became the first international golfer to win the U.S. Open. At the 1965 event held at the Bellerive Country Club in Missouri, he won an 18-hole playoff. It was also the only major championship Player had not won yet. At age 29, he became the third player to earn a career **Grand Slam**.

Player won his last major championship on the PGA Tour at The Masters in 1978. He started the final round seven strokes behind the leader. He recorded a **birdie** on seven of the last 10 holes to win the **green jacket** by one stroke.

Gary Player is the only golfer to win the Grand Slam on the PGA Tour and the Champions Tour.

> **"Every sport evolves. Every sport gets bigger and more athletic, and you have to keep up."**
>
> Tiger Woods

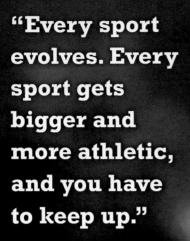

Sports Illustrated selected Tiger Woods as the 1996 and 2000 Sportsman of the Year. He became the first athlete to win the award more than once.

Player Profile

BORN Eldrick "Tiger" Woods was born on December 30, 1975, in Cypress, California.

FAMILY Woods was born to Earl and Kultida Woods. He has two half-brothers, Earl Jr. and Kevin, and a half-sister named Royce. Woods married Elin Nordegren in October 2004. They divorced in 2010. They have a daughter named Sam and a son named Charlie.

EDUCATION Woods attended Stanford University in 1994. He left after two years to become a professional golfer.

AWARDS Woods has won 14 major championships. He won the PGA Tour Rookie of the Year Award in 1996. He was the PGA Player of the Year in 1997, 1999, 2000, 2001, 2002, 2003, 2005, 2006, 2007, and 2009. He won the Vardon Trophy in 1999, 2000, 2001, 2002, 2003, 2005, 2007, and 2009. Woods was named the Associated Press Athlete of the Decade for the 2000s.

Tiger Woods

Turned pro: 1996

Early Years

When Tiger Woods was a baby, he watched his father practice golfing. Woods shot a 48 during a nine-hole game when he was 3 years old. He was featured in *Golf Digest* at age 5. Woods won the Optimist International Junior tournament six times by the age of 15. Woods became the youngest player ever to win the U.S. Junior Amateur championship in 1991.

Woods played in his first professional tournament in 1992. He played in three PGA Tour events in 1993. Woods won the U.S. Amateur Championship in 1994 when he was 18 years old. He became the youngest player to win the event.

Developing Skills

Woods played on the Stanford University golf team for two years. He was named the Jack Nicklaus College Player of the Year in 1996. He left school and became a professional golfer in August 1996. Woods won his first professional tournament at the 1996 Las Vegas International. He won his first major championship at The Masters in 1997. Woods set the all-time scoring record at the tournament. He finished 18 strokes under **par**. At age 21, Woods became the youngest player ever to win The Masters.

In 1997, Woods became the youngest player to reach the top of the Official World Golf Ranking. Woods has been ranked number one for a record total of 623 weeks during his career. He has won 77 PGA Tour events. Only Sam Snead has won more PGA tournaments. Woods has won 14 major championships. Jack Nicklaus is the only golfer to have won more major championships.

Tiger Woods

Greatest Moment

Woods won the British Open in 2000 when he was 24 years old. The victory made Woods the youngest golfer ever to complete the career Grand Slam.

At the 2008 U.S. Open, Woods sunk a birdie putt on the 18th hole to force a playoff against Rocco Mediate. The two golfers were still tied after another 18 holes. Woods won his 14th major championship on the first **sudden death** hole. After the tournament, Woods revealed he had played with an injured knee and a stress fracture in his left leg.

Between 2000 and 2001, Tiger Woods won all four Grand Slam tournaments in a row. This feat is now known as the Tiger Slam.

> "Confidence is the most important single factor in this game, and no matter how great your natural talent, there is only one way to obtain and sustain it: work."

Jack Nicklaus

Jack Nicklaus finished in the top 10 in 243 of the 357 professional events he played in between 1962 and 1979.

Player Profile

BORN Jack William Nicklaus was born on January 21, 1940, in Columbus, Ohio.

FAMILY Nicklaus was born to Charlie and Helen Nicklaus. He married Barbara Bash. They have five children: Jack II, Steve, Nancy, Gary, and Michael.

EDUCATION Nicklaus attended Ohio State University.

AWARDS Nicklaus won 18 major championships. He was named the PGA Player of the Year in 1967, 1972, 1973, 1975, and 1976. He was inducted into the World Golf Hall of Fame in 1974. Nicklaus received the PGA Tour Lifetime Achievement Award in 2008.

Jack Nicklaus

Turned pro: 1961

Early Years

Jack Nicklaus developed a love for many sports from his father Charlie. Nicklaus began playing golf when he was 10 years old. He scored a 51 during the first nine holes he played. Nicklaus soon began working with coach Jack Grout at the Scioto Country Club. He was 12 years old when he won the Ohio State Junior Championships in 1952. Nicklaus won the event five years in a row.

Nicklaus won the Ohio State Open at age 16. The next year, he won his first national tournament at the U.S. National Jaycees Championship. He also qualified for his first U.S. Open that year. Nicklaus won the U.S. Amateur Open for the first time in 1959. In 1960, he finished second at the U.S. Open. He shot a 282 at the tournament that year. This was a record for the best score by an amateur at the event. Nicklaus became a professional golfer in 1961.

Jack Nicklaus

Greatest Moment

Nicklaus was tied for first place with Arnold Palmer and Gary Player after the first two rounds at The Masters in 1965. In the third round, Nicklaus scored a birdie on five of the first eight holes and tied a course record by shooting a 64. He had an eight stroke lead heading into the final round. Nicklaus set a tournament record with a final score of 271. He won the event by nine strokes. It was a record for the largest margin of victory at The Masters. Both records stood for 22 years.

Developing Skills

Nicklaus earned his first professional victory at the U.S. Open in 1962. He defeated Arnold Palmer in an 18-hole playoff. Nicklaus won The Masters and the PGA Championship in 1963. Nicklaus won his first British Open in 1966 by one stroke. He became the fourth golfer to complete the career Grand Slam.

Nicklaus won 73 PGA Tour events during his career. He won 18 major championships, which is more than any other golfer. He won more money than any other player on the PGA Tour eight times. Nicklaus is tied with Arnold Palmer for the longest streak of winning at least one PGA Tour tournament in consecutive years, at 17.

Jack Nicklaus joined the Champions Tour in 1990. He has the record for most major championships victories on that tour, with eight.

> "Confidence in golf means being able to concentrate on the problem at hand with no outside interference."

Tom Watson

Tom Watson was named Golfer of the Decade for the 1980s. During those 10 years, he won 19 events and finished in the top 10 at 86 tournaments.

Tom Watson

Turned pro: 1971

Early Years

Tom Watson's father Ray was a **scratch golfer**. He was a member of the Kansas City Country Club. Watson began playing golf when he was 6 years old. He played many rounds with his father and also met Stan Thirsk at the country club. Thirsk was Watson's coach for many years.

Watson was the Missouri State Amateur Champion from 1968 to 1971. He later joined the Stanford University golf team. After graduating from university in 1971, Watson joined the PGA Tour.

Developing Skills

In 1974, Watson won his first PGA event at the Western Open. He nearly won his first major at the U.S. Open that year as well. Watson had a one stroke lead entering the final round at the U.S. Open. He shot a 79 on the final day and finished tied for fifth place. Watson won his second PGA Tour event at the Byron Nelson Classic in 1975. Two weeks later he competed in his first British Open. He won the tournament in an 18-hole playoff. It was his first major championship victory.

Watson won 39 PGA Tour events during his career, including eight majors. He won The Masters in 1977 and 1981, and he won the U.S. Open in 1982. From 1977 to 1980, Watson won more money than any other player on the PGA Tour. He was the top money winner again in 1984. Watson competed on the U.S. Ryder Cup teams in 1977, 1981, 1983, and 1989. He was captain of the team in 1993. Watson now plays on the Champions Tour. He has won 13 events and five major championships on this tour.

Tom Watson

Greatest Moment

The 1977 British Open is known as the "Duel in the Sun." The event was played in Scotland, and the weather was hot and sunny. After three rounds, Watson and Jack Nicklaus shot identical scores of 68, 70, and 65. They entered the final round tied for the lead. The two golfers took turns leading throughout the day. On the 17th hole, Watson took a one stroke lead after hitting a birdie. Nicklaus then made a 60-foot putt on the 18th hole to tie the game. Finally, Watson sunk a three-foot putt for a birdie to win the championship. It was Watson's second victory at the British Open. His score of 268 set a tournament record.

Tom Watson was almost 60 years old when he played in the British Open in 2009. He had not won a major tournament in 26 years. Watson lost the tournament in a playoff and finished in second place.

25

Greatest Moments

1911
John McDermott becomes the first golfer born in the United States to win the U.S. Open.

1922
Walter Hagen becomes the first golfer born in the U.S. to win the British Open.

1945
Byron Nelson wins 18 tournaments in one year. During the year, he sets a record with 19 consecutive rounds with a score below 70.

1954
Sam Snead defeats Ben Hogan by one stroke in a playoff to win The Masters.

1900   1910   1920   1930   1940   1950

1929
British businessman Samuel Ryder presents a trophy to the captain of Great Britain's team for winning the second Ryder Cup.

1930
Bobby Jones wins the U.S. Amateur, the British Amateur, the U.S. Open, and the British Open in the same year.

1935 – The Shot Heard 'Round the World

When: April 7, 1935

Where: Augusta, Georgia

Gene Sarazen hits a **double eagle** on the 15th hole in the final round of The Masters. The shot from 235 yards (215 m) tied Sarazen for the lead. Sarazen and Craig Wood remained tied at the end of the round. They played a 36-hole playoff the next day, and Sarazen won by five strokes.

When: June 18, 2000

Where: Pebble Beach, California

Tiger Woods scores a 272 at the U.S. Open at the Pebble Beach Golf Links. He finishes 12 strokes under par for the tournament. This is the first time a golfer finishes the U.S. Open with a score below par in double digits. He is the only player to finish the tournament under par and wins by 13 strokes. It sets a record for largest victory in a major championship.

1966
Jack Nicklaus becomes the first golfer to win The Masters two years in a row.

1977
Tom Watson defeats Jack Nicklaus by one shot at the British Open "Duel in the Sun."

1960   1970   1980   1990   2000

When: April 13, 1986

Where: Augusta, Georgia

Heading into The Masters in 1986, Jack Nicklaus was 46 and had not won a major event in six years. He had not won a PGA Tour event in two years. He shoots a 69 in the third round and starts the final day five strokes behind the leader. He then scores a 65 on the final day to win The Masters by one stroke. This was the sixth time Nicklaus had won The Masters, which is more times than any other golfer.

When: June 19, 2011

Where: Bethesda, Maryland

Rory McIlroy from Northern Ireland shoots a 65 to take the lead at the 2011 U.S. Open. He records a score in the 60s in all four rounds and leads the tournament. McIlroy sets a tournament record with a score of 268 to win his first major championship. In March 2012, McIlroy becomes the world's number one ranked golfer.

Write a Biography

Life Story

A person's life story can be the subject of a book. This kind of book is called a biography. Biographies often describe the lives of people who have achieved great success. These people may be alive today, or they may have lived many years ago. Reading a biography can help you learn more about a great person.

Get the Facts

Use this book, and research in the library and on the Internet, to find out more about your favorite golfer. Learn as much about this player as you can. How many tournaments did this person play in? What are his or her statistics in important categories? Has this person set any records? Also, be sure to write down key events in the person's life. What was this person's childhood like? What has he or she accomplished? Is there anything else that makes this person special or unusual?

Use the Concept Web

A concept web is a useful research tool. Read the questions in the concept web on the following page. Answer the questions in your notebook. Your answers will help you write a biography.

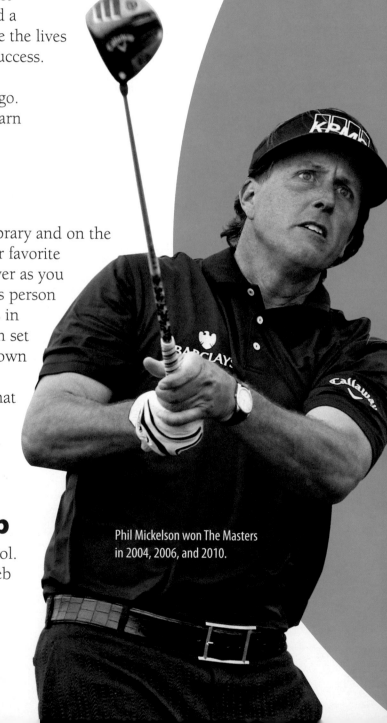

Phil Mickelson won The Masters in 2004, 2006, and 2010.

Concept Web

- What did you learn from the books you read in your research?
- Would you suggest these books to others?
- Was anything missing from these books?

- Where does this individual currently reside?
- Does he or she have a family?

- Where and when was this person born?
- Describe his or her parents, siblings, and friends.
- Did this person grow up in unusual circumstances?

Your Opinion

Adulthood

Childhood

WRITING A BIOGRAPHY

Main Accomplishments

Help and Obstacles

Work and Preparation

- What is this person's life's work?
- Has he or she received awards or recognition for accomplishments?
- How have this person's accomplishments served others?

- Did this individual have a positive attitude?
- Did he or she receive help from others?
- Did this person have a mentor?
- Did this person face any hardships?
- If so, how were the hardships overcome?

- What was this person's education?
- What was his or her work experience?
- How does this person work; what is the process he or she uses?

29

Know your STUFF!

1 How many holes are there in a typical round of golf?

2 How many times was Walter Hagen captain of the American Ryder Cup team?

3 Who is known as the inventor of the modern golf swing?

4 What do Arnold Palmer's fans call themselves?

5 What four tournaments did Bobby Jones win in 1930?

6 What is it called when a player wins all four major championship events during their career?

7 What did Sam Snead use to make golf clubs when he was a child on his family farm?

8 Which two golfers were trading leads during the "Duel in the Sun"?

9 How old was Tiger Woods when he completed the career Grand Slam?

10 Who hit the "Shot heard 'round the world" during The Masters in 1935?

ANSWERS: 1. 18 **2.** Six **3.** Byron Nelson **4.** Arnie's Army **5.** The U.S. Amateur, The British Amateur, The U.S. Open, and the British Open **6.** A Grand Slam **7.** Tree branches **8.** Tom Watson and Jack Nicklaus **9.** 24 **10.** Gene Sarazen

Key Words

birdie: a score of one less than par on a golf hole

blacksmith: someone who shapes iron by heating it up and hitting it with a hammer

British Open: a major golf tournament held every year in Great Britain, also known as The Open Championship

caddy: a person who assists a golfer and carries his or her bag of golf clubs

club professional: a professional who works at a golf club giving lessons and representing the golf club at tournaments

double eagle: a score of three less than par on a golf hole

Grand Slam: winning all four major golf tournaments

green jacket: a prize handed out every year to the winner of The Masters

hazards: obstacles golfers must try to avoid on a hole, such as water and sand

hook: a golf shot that does not fly in a straight line, curving to the left for a right-handed golfer and to the right for a left-handed golfer

match play: a competition where one point is awarded for having the lowest score on a hole and the player with the most points wins

par: the number of strokes expected to be used to complete a hole or a round

PGA Championship: a major golf tournament hosted every year in the U.S. by the PGA

Professional Golfers' Association (PGA) Tour: a series of tournaments and events for professional golfers

putting green: a smooth area of grass surrounding a hole on the golf course

rough: areas of long grass along a golf hole

Ryder Cup: a tournament held every two years between a team of golfers from the U.S. and a team of golfers from Europe

scratch golfer: a player who has the ability to score par or better during a round of golf

shafts: the long handles of golf clubs

stroke: a swing of the golf club

sudden death: additional holes to a round where the first player to take the lead after a hole wins the game

tee: a small peg where a golf ball is placed to sit above the ground for the first shot of a hole

The Masters Tournament: a major golf tournament held every year at the Augusta National Golf Club in Augusta, Georgia

ticker tape parade: a parade where large amounts of shredded paper are thrown into the air

tryout: a test of ability to join a team

U.S. Open: a major golf tournament held each year by the United States Golf Association

Vardon Trophy: an award handed out each year to the golfer with the lowest average score during a season

Index

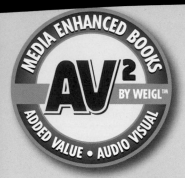

Log on to www.av2books.com

AV² by Weigl brings you media enhanced books that support active learning. Go to www.av2books.com, and enter the special code found on page 2 of this book. You will gain access to enriched and enhanced content that supplements and complements this book. Content includes video, audio, weblinks, quizzes, a slide show, and activities.

AV² Online Navigation

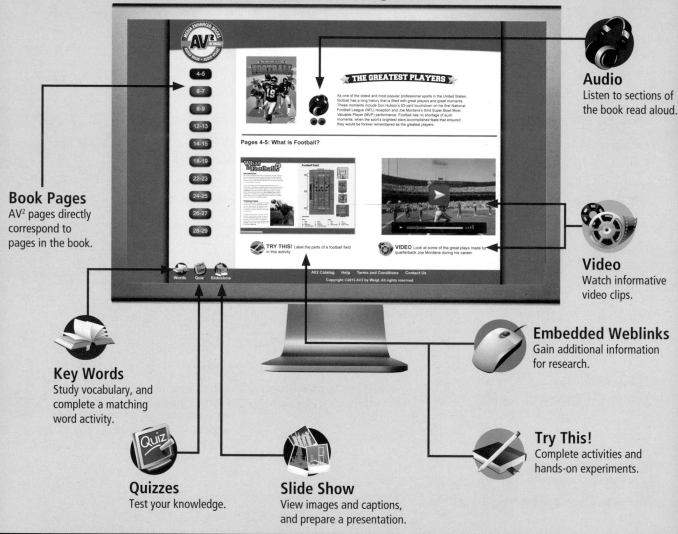

Audio
Listen to sections of the book read aloud.

Book Pages
AV² pages directly correspond to pages in the book.

Video
Watch informative video clips.

Embedded Weblinks
Gain additional information for research.

Key Words
Study vocabulary, and complete a matching word activity.

Try This!
Complete activities and hands-on experiments.

Quizzes
Test your knowledge.

Slide Show
View images and captions, and prepare a presentation.

AV² was built to bridge the gap between print and digital. We encourage you to tell us what you like and what you want to see in the future.

Sign up to be an AV² Ambassador at www.av2books.com/ambassador.

Due to the dynamic nature of the Internet, some of the URLs and activities provided as part of AV² by Weigl may have changed or ceased to exist. AV² by Weigl accepts no responsibility for any such changes. All media enhanced books are regularly monitored to update addresses and sites in a timely manner. Contact AV² by Weigl at 1-866-649-3445 or av2books@weigl.com with any questions, comments, or feedback.